Top Ten Checkride Tips

Kenny Keller & Dan "Taz" Christman

Copyright © 2018 Kenny Keller & Dan "Taz" Christman

All rights reserved.

ISBN-10: 1985338734
ISBN-13: 978-1985338739

DEDICATION

Dedicated to all those that suffer from the hype created by others about the dreaded, Helicopter Checkride! If you apply yourself, remember that we learn through repetition, go over the content repeatedly. Use our checkride tips to keep yourself calm, you will do just fine!

CONTENTS

	Acknowledgments	i
1	Start three weeks in advance	Pg 9
2	Prepare with the Practical Test Standards	Pg 13
3	Go through the requirements and pilot logbook in detail	Pg 17
4	Maintenance Logbooks, MMEL, MEL, Kinds of Equipment List	Pg 25
5	Cement your knowledge through repetition	Pg 31
6	Be an hour early	Pg 35
7	Lay out all your documents	Pg 39
8	Know that the checkride is hype	Pg 43
9	Answer like you are in court	Pg 51
10	I failed my first helicopter checkride	Pg 53
11	Additional	Pg 55
12	From The Examiners…	Pg 59
	About The Authors	Pg 65

ACKNOWLEDGMENTS

We'd like to say a special thank you to Taz Christman for helping us develop our instrument online course.. We have known Taz for a couple of years. He's from Indiana, flies in Las Vegas, and flies full-time for the Air Force. He is an airplane instructor, helicopter instructor, and an all-around nice and humble guy. He's done so many things in his career, and I don't know how he does all the things that he does. He has been instrumental in helping us get the instrument training course going, by recording videos for us. He's done 25 videos for our instrument online course, and he does a phenomenal job. Taz Christman is the 2018 Flight Instructor of the Year! That's on a national level! We just want to say thank you to Taz for everything he's done for us.

We would also like to give special thanks to DPEs Matt Binner (Airwork Las Vegas) and Patrick Edenfield (Mar-Les Helicopter Service) for providing checkride trends for both Private, Commercial and CFI checkrides over the past couple years.

The link to the instrument pilot course that Taz helped us build is www.joininstrumentpilot.com. The link for Helicopter Online Ground School www.helicopterground.com. We also have a course for people interested in remote piloting at www.joinremotepilot.com. The course is up and ready to help you get that remote pilot certification. **Remote Pilot 107 Online**, our new book, hit Amazon's top seller in the number one spot! It is available for you now at www.amazon.com/author/kennykeller.

Introduction

I'm Kenny Keller, creator of **Helicopter Online Ground School**. In this short read we cover our top ten checkride tips. These tips are very basic, but that's the key. People screw up on checkrides because of very basic things.

As we get into our tips for the checkride, we want to add our normal disclaimer. Remember that it is up to you to know the procedures for your aircraft and your environment. We're going to provide some tips, some things that I've seen in 20 years of instructing, that are very basic. These may be basic, but they are things that I don't want you to overlook.

Chapter 1
Start three weeks in advance

It doesn't matter whether it is taking you three months, six months, two years, four years, or more. The time varies for anybody going for a checkride. You are preparing the whole time you are flying. Your instructor is doing his job working with you. You're working through the PTS, and you're doing what you are supposed to be doing. So often, it is the last-minute issues that bite people in the rear.

When I say to start three weeks in advance, I mean to start getting the materials ready three weeks in advance of the day of the checkride. I am always amazed that students will show up to a checkride without CURRENT Aeronautical Charts, FAR/AIM, PTS or Chart Supplements (formally A/FD).

There is nothing worse than on the night before the checkride thinking, "I don't have a chart. I don't have an E6B. I don't have this, I don't have that." It is the most horrible feeling in the world for you and a horrible feeling for your instructor because you both look unprepared showing up at the checkride trying to sneak through saying, "Well, I couldn't get this in time," or "I forgot that." It just doesn't look good. If it is required, you will not be able to take the test.

You want to show up at the checkride prepared. I just picked three weeks as a general rule. I used to say one or two weeks, but I love the number three. You should have everything that you need for the day of the checkride three weeks in advance. You should have all the tools and things that we talk about three weeks in advance of that checkride. Everything you need is listed in the PTS (page 1-xi) under "Applicant's Practical Test Checklist". We will provide a copy of the checklist in the Appendix.

Much of these items are now available digitally and can be updated within a few minutes. The FAA has now approved the use of these digital products for checkrides, but I would check with your DPE as to what he expects. There are a few "old hats" out there that might still want you to demonstrate on paper, as a backup.

A note on the use of digital products. Tablets have an uncanny knack for over heating or running out of battery right at the most inopportune time. Have a plan ready should this happen. I had a student who was using his iPad for his instrument check. Halfway through the first approach, it over heated. He had to land and print out the subsequent approach plates. Lucky for him his examiner was being generous. That might not always be the case.

Kenny Keller & Dan "Taz" Christman

Chapter 2
Prepare with the Practical Test Standards
(Soon to be the ACS)

We recently spoke with the FAA and asked about the Airman Certification Standards (ACS) for helicopter ratings. The fixed wing side of the house changed over about three years ago. The FAA said that the ACS is still a ways off in the future for rotorcraft. If you're reading this a few years down the road, it may have since become the ACS. Regardless, the information contained in this chapter is still 100% valid.

I've learned that there are instructors who don't use the Practical Test Standards (PTS), and thus students who don't use and have never heard of the PTS. If the PTS is not one of the first books your instructor pulls out, then it might be time to find a new school. The instructor and you should be going through the PTS throughout your training, starting from the first lesson. One of the first questions an examiner usually asks is, do you have a PTS. This is dead giveaway for not being prepared if you do not have one in your possession.

The most pivotal time to really get into the PTS is in those last several weeks before your ride. There is no mystery to the checkride. The PTS is your test! The "Examiner's Practical Test Checklist" tells you exactly what he is going to test you on. There are some mandatory items that must be tested. They are clearly stated in the PTS. No excuses for not knowing those items. It also spells out the requirements for add-on pilots. I don't want to go into a big thing on the PTS because we could say a lot about the PTS, but you should be using it. You should be working through it.

I will tell one story on that. This tip is to show you the importance of preparing with the PTS. I went to Michigan to fly the testing for a supplemental type certification. I met a gentleman who had been an examiner for 40 years. He asked me what I did for a living. I said, "Well, I have this little ground school where I teach people how to prepare for a checkride with online video. I based it all on the PTS."

He shook my hand and said, "Thank you very much. You know what? As a 40-year examiner, do you know how many times people show up for checkrides and have never used the PTS?" He continued, "I had a guy show up for a CFI checkride, and he had never used a PTS in his career. I told him I wasn't going to give him the checkride."

The examiner said that the guy then begged him for the checkride saying, "Yeah. I'm sorry. I knew I should have been using the PTS."

The examiner did end up letting the guy take the checkride, and the guy passed. But the examiner told me, "Kenny, the thing I've seen, again as a 40-year examiner, is that many people don't use the PTS when they should. Thank you for starting a school and basing it on the PTS."

Therefore, if you are not using it yet in your training, then you need to start. Many times, I'll ask a student to take out their PTS and look something up. They pull it out and you can tell they haven't looked at it once! Pages are still nice and neat. No creases in the spine. No notes are tabs for quick reference. You are doing yourself a disservice if you are not using it throughout your training.

I know these are basic tips. Generally, the basic things are what trip people up on checkrides. You've got weeks, months, or maybe even years that you prepare with flight and ground training. Don't blow it by missing something stupid on the day of your checkride.

As you read through the PTS, notice the notes in each Area of Operation and under each Task. For example, under Area of Operation I. Preflight Preparation it says "the examiner shall develop a scenario based on real time weather to evaluate tasks C, D, E and F".

So when the examiner says, "Tell me how you collected your weather for this flight today, and what information you looked at"…

As you can see under Task C, you must exhibit knowledge of METAR, TAF, and FA, Surface Analysis chart, radar summary chart, etc. Be prepared to give the examiner all the weather information.

Task D requires the examiner to make sure the applicant can complete a navigation log and simulates filing a VFR flight plan. This is a very weak area most examiners see because a lot of helicopter CFIs do not make their students file a flight plan during their entire private pilot training. In today's digital age, there is no reason students should not know how to file, open and close flight plans. Most students have never actually filed a flight plan with FSS, opened the flight plan, and closed the flight plan. It's even easier nowadays. You can do it all from your smart phone through texting. Yes the examiner still expects you to be able to explain how to do the phone briefing and filing, as well as RCO and VOR communications procedures while airborne. However the new kid on the block is the text messaging program through www.1800wxbrief.com.

Chapter 3
Go through the requirements and pilot logbook in detail

I have a great story for this tip from a checkride that I was doing last fall. I've known this gentleman for a while. He's very smart. He's a jet pilot. He flies IFR all the time. He's a 135 trainer. He already had a private helicopter add-on, and he was doing a commercial helicopter add-on to all his fixed-wing stuff. Smart guy. Sharp individual. He studied hard and knew the material. We were about a week away from the checkride, and I said, "Let's sit down and go through your pilot's logbook."

He said, "Oh, I have all of the requirements."

And I said, "Well, I know, but I want you to sit down and go through them with me." He grumbled, and he didn't like it. I said, "You know what? Would you just do this? This, is what I do. I want to go through the requirements with you." He didn't want to do it, but he did.

We got out the FAR/AIM manual and looked at the requirements for commercial pilot. We opened his logbook and put it next to the requirements. I told him that we would go through them together. I said, "We're going to go through this like we are kindergarteners or first graders.

I'm not insulting your intelligence, but I'm going to go through here step-by-step, and you are going to verify that you have these things in your logbook." He didn't like it, but he did it.

When we started going through things, we came across a requirement that was something like "two-hour cross-country day VFR flight." I asked him where that was in his logbook, and he replied, "Uh. I have 1.8."

I said, "Well, this says 2.0."

"But I flew with an examiner who prepped me for this before I came to you, so you could finish me off, and he said that was fine," he responded.

I replied, "Well, I know he's an examiner, but the book right here says 2.0, and you have 1.8."

He looked at it and kind of argued a little bit, but he finally agreed with me, "You know what? You're right." So, we had to go out and do another requirement. This guy had his act together. He's very smart. He flew with an examiner, but this examiner didn't take the time to open the book and make sure that, word-for-word, his student had exactly what was needed for that checkride. He went to the checkride and passed first time around.

The lesson here is that you need to open the logbook and go to the FAR/AIM. It doesn't matter whether it is private pilot, commercial pilot, instrument pilot, or whatever it is you are working on. You need to open your logbook and go through it step-by-step.

What we like to do is take something like a yellow highlighter and put a mark by those specific requirements in your logbook. If you are brand new to this, your logbook is not very big. If you are an add-on guy like this gentleman, a rated pilot with all kinds of rating flights, all kinds of aircraft, you will have a lot in your logbook.

When you go to your checkride, you must prove to the examiner that you have completed all the requirements and are eligible to take the test. What that means is he has to go through your logbook and see each of the requirements logged appropriately before he proceeds. The easier you make this for the examiner the better. Don't start out on the wrong foot, and make a huge ordeal out of finding the requirements.

I cannot stress enough how important it is for you to go through your logbook piece-by-piece and step-by-step with the FAR/AIM and make sure you have all the requirements logged in your logbook.

Make sure that your pages are totaled. Make sure that every page is signed. I have had an examiner come in and throw a logbook at me and say, "His pages aren't signed, and his hours aren't totaled. Did you know that? Did you even look at his logbook?" Well, how stupid did I look? That was me as a brand-new instructor. Mistakes happen even to experienced instructors.

All those little things like filling out the logbook, adding the pages, finding those requirements, do not overlook them. If you show up the day of the checkride and you don't have a requirement done, you can't take the test. No examiner will let you take the test if you don't have the requirements. It's just not going to happen.

Remember this is your checkride. Your instructors will do their best to prepare you, but they can overlook items too. Be methodical about your logbook. Your logbook is your career, make sure it looks like you care.

Gary Cleveland our chief pilot, recently shared a story about when he took a gentleman over to one of three examiners who we deal with quite routinely. The examiners have a lot of similarities, and they have some differences. Gary took the student to the examiner over in Toledo. The student had actually been signed off by a CFI from another state and had just moved here and wanted to finish. Gary was just riding with him for insurance purposes in the aircraft. This examiner, just like the other two we've used, didn't want to leaf through and find something. You may think you have it all squared away, but they're going to say, "Point to it." They'll pick out a couple of random things that are part of your aeronautical experience in Part 61, and they will say, "Show me this," or "Show me that." They want you to be able to leaf through and point it out to them.

Gary had not gone down through the logbook with this particular student since he was just riding with him for insurance purposes. The examiner went to look at the student's endorsement to take the checkride. The student said that he had already had the three hours of checkride prep. He said that his CFI had just emailed him that endorsement, and the student had printed the email. This got complicated, and Gary was glad that he was not the one recommending the student, because he likes everything to be squared away.

The examiner had to get on the phone with the FAA and it took a little while. The FAA got back with him and said that they could proceed with that endorsement since it was emailed and signed by his instructor, but they wanted it printed, cut out, and taped into his logbook. There's no sense going to a checkride and taking a chance like that. Just have it all done and have it all done right, with all the endorsements that you need.

Endorsements are huge. The FAA AC-65 will tell the CFI exactly how these endorsements should be worded. Sometimes the examiner will want something re-worded to match that circular.
Make sure the endorsements are for the correct category of aircraft. Many preprinted logbooks refer to the sections dealing with airplanes. Make sure they are specific to helicopters.

Here is an example:

Flight proficiency/practical test: §§ 61.103(f), 61.107(b)(1), and 61.109.
I certify that [First name, MI, Last name] has received the required training in accordance with §§ 61.107(b)(1) and 61.109. I have determined [he or she] is prepared for the [name of] practical test.

The problem with the endorsement above is that it specifically states that the student received the training in accordance with 61.107(b)(1), which refers to the requirements for airplanes. It should be 61.107(b)(3). Logbook manufactures are starting to make the logbooks more general, but watch out if you have a "legacy" logbook.

When Gary was preparing for his CFI checkride, we went through everything the day before the checkride. Gary's medical had been in and out of his pocket so much that we couldn't read the date on it. We called the examiner who said that he had to be able to read the date on it. Gary thought, "Oh, this is the day before. What are we going to do?" Luckily, we had gone down that road to check and didn't go all the way to Toledo with all that fuel and aircraft time just to get sent back.

Gary was able to get online with the FAA, and they were able to find the record of his medical and send him a printable email so that we could print off another one. This tip is important. Be sure to go through everything like a kindergartener. It doesn't matter if you are going for your first private checkride or your commercial CFI instrument checkride. Whichever checkride you are going to, don't forget the basics.

We are passionate about this stuff. Many of you out there have come up the hard bumpy road. I feel most people who have become helicopter pilots have. For most people, it wasn't handed to them. For most people, it was very expensive. Most people have struggled through the ratings. They've struggled through the ground school. They've struggled with something in the flight. I have had every single stupid thing that can happen to a person happen to me. It's experience. Experience is how we learn. Learning is just that, a change in behavior as the result of experience. It's not that I'm the smartest guy on the planet. It's because I've made all the dumb mistakes, and I've had to struggle, beg, borrow, "steal" and do everything necessary to get my ratings. I can say I am well "experienced".

The more ratings you get as a pilot, the more important it is to correctly log and annotate the requirements in your logbook. The problem is that as your logbook gets bigger over time with more ratings and more aircraft, that stuff gets hard to go back and find. This makes that much more imperative that you correctly log and annotate all your training. Make your logbook look the way you want your career; neat, legible, correct, and complete. Take pride in it. To steal a quote from the rifleman's creed, This is my logbook. "There are many like it, but this one is mine."

Chapter 4
Maintenance Logbooks, MMEL, MEL, Kinds of Equipment List

We've always tabbed the common inspections in the aircraft maintenance log. But we recently had an examiner who brought up tabbing. He said that there has been some talk amongst the examiners at their meetings that they are starting to ask questions that people aren't used to hearing because everybody tabs everything. Examiners have gotten wise to that strategy, so instead of asking all the same stuff, they ask you for something in the aircraft logbook that they don't normally ask because they want to see what a person does.

The examiner is required to ask the applicant for the standard inspection in order to verify that the aircraft is indeed airworthy.

Be sure you can identify and locate the following:

AVIATES
    Annual (12 months)
    VOR Check (every 30 Days if used for IFR)
    I00 Hour or Progressive inspection (for hire or instruction)
    Airworthiness Directives
    Transponder (24 months 91.413)
    ELT (12 months if installed)
    Static inspection (Pitot/Static – 24months 91.411)

We are all trained to find the 100-hour and the transponder and altimeter, but they might ask for something that is not normally asked.

This came up in one of our recent checkrides, and that came straight from the examiner. He said, "Well, there's a flipside to tabbing everything." Be prepared for him to ask for something not tabbed. We open that aircraft logbook and have those inspections tabbed. We know the things the examiner will normally ask to see. But just be prepared. Don't rely on tabs only. Make sure, as a student, that you go through the aircraft logbook. Make sure, as an instructor, that you're going through the aircraft logbook with your students.

Even though I had a great instructor, one of the reasons I failed my first checkride was because every time we would go to look at the logbooks, they were locked up in the hangar. The mechanic wasn't there. This continued to happen. When I failed my private pilot that first time, it was because he had said, "Let's take a look at the aircraft log books," and I had to tell him that they were over in the maintenance area.

The examiner told me to get the instructor and find the logbooks. The instructor brought them over to the examiner who asked to see the last 100-hour. I started flipping through. The examiner started tapping the table and huffing and puffing, and I could tell he was getting frustrated, so I said, "Honestly, I've never seen this book before."

He wasn't impressed. He said, "Well, keep digging. Keep looking." And that's one thing he hammered both myself and my instructor about after I failed.

The examiner said, "Well, it's no excuse. You should have found the logbooks prior to checkride day. Showing up for a checkride, having never seen the aircraft logbooks, is not good."

That was our biggest mistake on the private checkride that I failed. Understanding the aircraft logbooks and tabbing things is great, but make sure you understand whatever else is in there. If it's a newer aircraft, it's easy. If it's an aircraft that has been around for 30 years, like a lot of helicopters are, and it has 10,000, 12,000, 15,000 hours on it, those logbooks can get very complicated.

Another issue that has come up recently is inoperative equipment. 14 CFR § 91.213(d)(3) Inoperative instruments and equipment states:

"The inoperative instruments and equipment are -

> (i) Removed from the aircraft, the cockpit control placarded, and the maintenance recorded in accordance with § 43.9 of this chapter; or
>
> (ii) Deactivated and placarded "Inoperative." If deactivation of the inoperative instrument or equipment involves maintenance, it must be accomplished and recorded in accordance with part 43 of this chapter;"

A lot of older aircraft have "inoperative" equipment installed in the aircraft. Many examiners are now looking for these "inop" entries into the maintenance logbooks. Be sure if your aircraft has "inoperative" equipment you can locate the required logbook entry.

Another often confusing and overlooked knowledge area is that of Minimum Equipment List (MEL). Task B in the PTS requires the applicant to exhibit knowledge for procedures for determining airworthiness with inoperative instruments and equipment with and without an MEL. This is a very weak subject area with most applicants having a hard time explaining the difference between an MMEL and an MEL.

So what exactly is an **Minimum equipment list (MEL)**? A MEL as defined in Advisory Circular 91-67 is a precise listing of instruments, equipment, and procedures that allows an aircraft to be operated under specific conditions with inoperative equipment. The MEL is the specific inoperative equipment document for a particular make and model aircraft by serial and registration numbers.

The **master minimum equipment list (MMEL)** contains a list of items of equipment and instruments that may be inoperative on a specific type of aircraft. <u>This does not include a specific aircraft by registration number.</u> This is the basis for the development of an individual operator's MEL.

Obviously, most small General Aviation aircraft do not have a MEL. So how do we determine if we can proceed with a flight if we have inoperative equipment. Most students will quote 14 CFR 91.205 where it lists the required Day/Night VFR and IFR equipment. But not all equipment listed in 91.205 covers each aircraft. For that we have to look at the aircraft's "Kinds of Operations List (KOL). As an example, let's look at the Robinson R22. In Section 2 it lists the "Kinds of Operation Limitations". Specifically VFR day is approved. For night however it adds some extra requirements over 91.205. VFR operation at night is permitted only when landing, navigation, instrument, and anti-collision lights are operational. Additionally, Orientation during night flight must be maintained by visual reference to ground objects illuminated solely by lights on the ground or adequate celestial illumination.

Kenny Keller & Dan "Taz" Christman

Chapter 5
Cement your knowledge through repetition

We know that we learn through repetition. We cement our knowledge through reviewing over and over again. When I failed my first checkride, not only did we have the logbook problem, we had other problems. The examiner asked me about settling with power. Back at that time, the memory aid was 30-20-10. Back then it was rate of descent 300 feet per minute or greater, using 20-100% power, airspeed less than 10. That's from the old basic helicopter handbook from 1978. That was the memory aid 20 years ago.

When the examiner asked me about settling with power, I tried to stumble through it and hem-hawed around, saying something like "rate of descent" and I got some parts correct. Then I said, "using full power." I wasn't very smooth with that settling of power. In turn, that's why you hear me harp on that over and over and over in ground school today.

After I failed, the examiner said, "You know, we had a problem with the logbooks. When I ask you a question, I need an answer quickly and confidently when it's something that could kill you, like settling with power. I want to hear the words '30-20-10, rate of descent 300 feet per minute or greater, power 20-100%. You said, 'using all power' or something like that. You were not confident in your response!
You cement your knowledge by going through everything that you need to use, using all the materials that we recommend inside Helicopter Online Ground School, and going through them over and over again. And when I say, cement your knowledge through repetition. Remember that. It is one thing when you're home studying by yourself and it's another thing when you're with your instructor, whom you get comfortable with over a period of time. It's a different thing the day you show up to the checkride.

The nerves come into play the day of the checkride. It's a different place, and it's a guy you've never met before. Your knowledge has got to be better than when you were with your instructor, and that knowledge has got to be better than it was when you were home studying. You go over it, and you go over it. If you want to be successful through the checkride, you do it through cementing your knowledge by going over and over and over the materials. You want to know it so darn well that you're not going to forget it.

One of our first students that we talk about all the time is Jamie. He did his private and commercial with us. Jamie went through our videos over and over, and over again. He said, "Kenny, I went through them all a minimum of probably three times."

I'm not saying you have got to go through every video three times, but the people who have done the best on their checkrides tell us they went through every single video. They don't come in and just grab a chunk here and grab a chunk there. If they tell us they struggled, we go in and look to see how many videos they completed. If you only use 10 out of 100 videos, then expect to only get 10% of the knowledge. Its important to apply yourself completely.

We learn from repetition. Go over and over and over and over the material!

Experts say we learn 75% from seeing, 13 % from hearing, 6 % from touching, 3 % from tasting, and 3 % from smelling.

Watch the videos inside Helicopter Online Ground School and you will be using the two biggest senses. Add in note taking and you will retain even more.

A great example of cementing your knowledge is by knowing your systems cold. Task G in the PTS says the examiner must pick at least 3 systems to discuss. There are not that many systems on most GA helicopters, so know all of them. Look at the systems description in the POH/RFM and go out to the helicopter and be able to point things out. If you read it in the book that is rote learning, but if you can explain it at the helicopter and why the system works a certain way, then you have achieved the correlation level of learning, which is what the examiner is looking for.

Be sure you know your way around the POH or Flight Manual. A lot of schools have pre-printed performance and weight balance data sheets to be filled out before each flight. Examiners want to see students use the actual POH. Don't be the guy who can't find the OGE (Out Of Ground Effect) chart in the Flight Manual. Examiners can see the stress building as students nervously flip through the POH trying to find a certain chart. When students can confidently flip right to the charts, they keep the checkride atmosphere positive and keep moving right along. This same thing applies to the FAR/AIM. On a check ride, you have to use the actual publication. The applicant must reference the FAA publication, manufacture handbook, etc.

Chapter 6
Be an hour early

You're taught this from day one. You should never be late anywhere you go, especially when it is something important. When I first got started as a brand-new instructor, the place I was working said, "Hey, go out and fly with the examiner for an hour so you guys get to know each other." And I thought that was great. It was only the second place I had worked. It was the first time meeting this examiner that I've now used for 20 years.

He said, "make sure you're here on time. And make sure you have everything you need because that's the problem that I have." And, over the years seeing it, he gets aggravated when you are not there on time. And the checkrides just don't go as well. Therefore, my advice is to be there an hour early. The earlier the better, so that you get there, you have time to add fuel if it's needed, you have time to take a breath.

You have time to get something to drink. You have time to go in and start laying things out.

I can tell you from my 20 years of experience that being late to a checkride is the quickest way to a not so good checkride. Chris Houser is one of our instructors. I've been flying with Chris forever. Chris had an awesome private pilot helicopter checkride. A couple of years later we went to do his commercial, and he had a lot of other things on his mind that day. For whatever reason, we left late. I remember kind of freaking out when we were getting over there. As we were getting closer and closer, I was thinking, "I'm never late. I am never late. I've never been late to a checkride with this examiner. Never."

I prewarned the examiner that we were on our way and that we might be a few minutes late. He said in a text message that it was all cool and that it was fine. But I can tell you what, showing up late, the whole checkride was just different. And I know deep down that he was aggravated because we weren't there on time.

Chris was already frustrated. This was the one where Chris got stuck on airplane and helicopter regulations, day and night, VFR, and Class G. When it got into that nitty-gritty, Chris worked himself into a hole. The examiner asked, "What's basic VFR?" All he wanted to hear was "three miles and a thousand feet." Chris had just worked himself into a tizzy at this point and couldn't answer. The examiner was looking at me going, "Oh, my gosh."

I'm in the background behind Chris and this goes on a for a while. The examiner then stated, "I'm just asking you basic VFR. What is basic VFR?" This goes on and he finally said, "Well, I'm going to go get a coffee. I'll be back," and he walked out.

We saved the checkride, but the only time I ever showed up late for a checkride, it sucked, and we barely got through it. It's three failures in 20 years, so I have a pretty good record on getting people through and knowing what it takes. As simple as being an hour early sounds to you, take my advice and be there an hour or more early. Showing up and being prepared looks good to the examiner.

I have had hours of sitting in on oral checkrides and knowing how these go. If you received your CFI rating in the last few years, you have very limited experience sitting in on students when they get their oral questioning of their checkride because things have changed. He also reminded us that I can relate to years of sitting in and listening to different students being questioned because they allowed me to be in the room.

I have always done what it takes for my students over the years, even when I went along for a checkride and it blew a majority of my day. I wasn't even charging them anything for it. When I was struggling as an instructor and needed the money, I still would never charge anyone to go for a checkride. An examiner would always let me sit in, and I went that extra mile so that I could sit in and see how the checkrides go.

I've been doing it a long time. I've sat in on hundreds of them, so I know what trips people up.

That's why I built **Helicopter Online Ground School**. It's years of experience, of me doing all the stupid stuff I've done. It's training a lot of people over the years, staying active as an instructor even when I was flying EMS or doing whatever else. I always go the extra mile for my students.

An Important note about showing up early is to remember what time zone you are in and what time zone your examiner is in. Taz had two students that he was taking for their Private checkride in Utah. Unfortunately, all three of them forgot the time zone change. Las Vegas is on Pacific time and Saint George Utah is on Mountain time. Of course this was the first time he had used this particular examiner. The checkride was scheduled at 0800, and it takes about an hour to fly from Vegas to Saint George. Forgetting about the time change, they planned to leave Las Vegas at 0630 giving them time to fuel the plane before they left and still get there 30 minutes early. As Murphy's Law states; "Anything that can go wrong will go wrong". The fuel truck took extra-long to get to the aircraft. They ended up departing closer to 0645 Vegas time. Which was 0745 in Utah. Hour flight up put them arriving at 0845. They did not realize the time error until after arrival. Not a good first impression. Luckily, the students where well prepared, and breezed through the ground portion. All was forgiven, but a valuable lesson was learned.

Chapter 7
Lay out all your documents
(nice and neat for the examiner)

This chapter is going to be full of "Taz Tech". While none of what I bring up is mandatory, they are the techniques that have worked for myself and my students over the years.

On the day of the exam you want to put your best foot forward. Show the examiner that you take your rating seriously. That starts with your appearance. The more professional the rating, the more professional you should look. This does not mean you need to show up in your Sunday best, but it's also not the time to show up in a tank top and flip flops. I'm not going to belabor the point, but if your outfit would fit nicely on "peopleofwalmart.com" you might want to rethink your selection.

Make sure you take the required items with you. I've had students show up to the checkride only to find out that they left their written test results, logbook, photo ID, medical, 8710, etc. at home. Especially don't forget the payment… in cash! I've seen it all. Don't be that guy! The night before, go through the applicant checklist in the PTS (appendix) and pack all the required items in your flight bag.

It's not on the checklist in the PTS, but make sure you know your FAA Tracking Number (FTN) and password. Your examiner will need your FTN to pull up your application. You will also be required to digitally sign your application most likely on his computer. To do that you need your log in ID and Password.

Top Ten Checkride Tips

Nothing annoys the examiner more than waiting for you to reset your password, or have to call the help number because you forgot your FTN. The quicker you can get him through the paperwork the better.

Speaking of getting through the paperwork quickly, we talked about being an hour early in the last chapter. Use that time wisely. Don't just sit there and wait for the examiner. If you have access to the testing room, get everything laid out for him.

Have all your paperwork laid out nice and neat. Have your Photo ID, Medical, and Student pilot certificate set aside ready for him to pick up. Have your logbook opened to the proper endorsements. Have the aircraft logbooks ready for inspection. Current weight and balance for both the simulated flight as well as the actual checkride flight. Be sure to have all your flight planning and weather information ready to go over. Finally have all your resources ready should you need to reference them. It's great to have a notebook for studying, but remember that the DPE can only except information from the FAA source data. I.E. Helicopter flying Handbook, POH/RFM, FAR/AIM etc. Have them laid out ready for use.

If you take nothing else away from this chapter, remember that if the examiner is waiting on you to provide him with information it will delay the beginning of the ride, and extend the entire day. A few minutes of prep go a long way.

One last Taz Tech, bring doughnuts! Okay, so this one isn't really required, but I've been bringing doughnuts to every check ride since my first Commercial check ride 20 years ago. Every time one of my examiners eats a doughnut, my student passes. I'm sure that has more to do with the actual check ride prep rather than the tasty goodness, but I'm not one to tempt fate.

Chapter 8
Know that the checkride is hype

This is one thing that Gary and I talk about that I'm not sure we've openly talked about on camera, or in any of our videos. This is what we think. I know that it's easy for us to say but, know that the checkride is hype. Don't take that the wrong way. Yes, you must perform, and there's a lot of things you have got to know. You must study. You have got to apply yourself. But if you do all of that and you do it right, you're going to go to the checkride and you're most likely going to pass.

You need to think back about how there is a lot of hype. In reality, most people, even the ones that are really scared, will say afterwards, "Wow. I did pretty well." Even though the flying always goes to heck the last couple of days before a checkride, I'm telling you that people usually do well. That's why I'd prefer not to fly with you one or two days before a checkride. I like to be finished two days in advance and you not even come in the day before the checkride. Sometimes you have got to come in to clean things up a little bit or give someone confidence, but I like to be done a day or two before you go see the examiner.

Those last couple days of prep, their flying and ground knowledge goes downhill. The harder you work and the harder you try, the more it sucks. And the day before the checkride, they can't fly worth a poop. I'm just telling you. Twenty years of watching this happen.

I think back to when I went through the Indiana Law Enforcement Academy. At that time, it was a tough academy. It was number four in the nation, and it was known to be a really tough academy. All the cops that I knew had me all jacked up before I went there. They have you so freaked out that the day you get there, your mind is blown.

I remember that they checked our blood pressure that day, and I was one of about twenty out of a group of a hundred. They said, "We have to check you guys out and get you guys calmed down. Your blood pressure is way too high. The rest of you can go." They told our group to sit in the room and calm down. They said that they would be back to check our blood pressure. I eventually passed. It was the first day of the Indiana Law Enforcement Academy, and it was a lot of hype. Yeah, it was hard. I had to study. I had to apply myself, but I got through it and did very well at the police academy. You can do the same thing with the checkride.

I had one student who really struggled in the oral. We did a ton of ground. He was prepared, but he let his nerves get to him, and it was one of the worst I have ever done. I was completely embarrassed. I couldn't believe he passed. The examiner even said, "Hey, when I go out in the aircraft, I'm going to make sure that he knows these things. You saw him struggle in the oral."

I said, "Yeah. He knows the info. He just has his head up his butt today."

The examiner continued, "I'm going to re-ask these questions while we're flying. I'm going to dig into all the hard stuff and the things that will kill you. I'm going to dig into those things while we are flying to make sure that he understands what is going to get him killed and how to avoid these problems. I have to make sure he can understand these things in the environment while he's flying."

And I agreed, "Hey, of course, fair game, of course." The guy passed, but afterwards he was angry because he had this horrible checkride. He was so mad, and I'm like, "Hey. You made it. Why are you so mad?"

He said, "Well, I've just never…" He was used to excelling in everything in his life, so the one time that things didn't go his way, his attitude just went completely south.

Gary recently said it is always about remaining calm. It is. It's about remaining calm on the checkride. It's about remaining calm in any thing you do in life. Becoming a pilot teaches you so many other things about being a person, and becoming a pilot improves things about you in other areas of your life. I've never openly used the statement that, "the checkride is just hype," and I don't want you to think that I'm just saying, "Oh, the checkride isn't any big deal." That's not what I'm saying. If you are prepared and you use these tips that we talk about. You study, you apply yourself, and you know the material, you are going to get through it.

I already mentioned earlier that it's just different when you're sitting across the table from that guy. Even our examiner, who is one of my long-time friends, all these hundreds of checkrides, has said, "I get nervous when I sit across from the FAA for my checkride. We all do."

And examiners know that you're nervous. Our examiners are pretty fair when somebody gets a little upset. They don't just slam you down and go, "You failed. Get out of here. You suck." It's not like that. If you are hyperventilating a little bit, or you're breathing heavy and getting all upset, usually they will go, "Hey, let's just take a minute. Go grab a cup of coffee. Take a walk outside if that's what you need to do." Normally, when an examiner sees you are freaking out, they will try to help you. They're not going to give you the checkride, but they will help you.

Gary next explains how a new examiner gave us detailed information on how the examiner was taught to administer the check ride.

Gary recalled, "Oh, you're talking about when he was going down through his checklist as an examiner. Kenny was allowed to sit in with me on my commercial. That was probably one of the last checkrides he was allowed to sit in on before they stopped allowing that.

"You were sitting in with me on my commercial checkride and the examiner said, 'Okay, I have a checklist I have got to follow. *Make student feel relaxed.* Okay. This is the refrigerator over here. We have drinks. The restrooms are down the hall.' And he said, 'I'm here to pass you today. I'm not here to fail you, so I really hope that we have the same goal of you leaving here with your certificate.'

"He made it clear that he wasn't a monster. His goal was to pass me if I met the standards. We both had the same goal, and we moved forward from there.

"Kenny's probably going to get to this, but the big thing to remember when the examiner asks those questions is to just be calm, think about the answer, and just answer that specific question. Don't turn the answer into a lecture. If he asks you about retreating blade stall, don't lead that into the helicopter's pitching up on the nose because of gyroscopic procession. And gyroscopic procession is this, and this is why, etc.. Let him ask the questions that should follow. Keep it simple. Think about your answers, and just give him the answer to the question he is asking. Don't go on and on, let him ask the next question."

Here's what I've seen in all these years doing checkrides, they suck the night before and people are nervous and freaked out. And after the checkride is finished, they go, "Wow, I did really well. I did good."

I say, "Well, nice. How did the flight go?"

And they reply, "The flight went great."

The examiner will say, "Nice job today."

It gives me goosebumps when you walk out of the oral saying it went great. Even when people suck the last one to two days before the checkride, their knowledge goes out the window, and their flying goes to Hell. They somehow get through the oral the majority of the time. If you do everything we tell you, you will be fine. You get there early. you have your stuff, you are prepared, and you have cemented your knowledge, then you have confidence. Most examiners are really cool. I'm not saying that there's not an examiner that might get a little crazy out there. We had one that I would never use again because he went overboard the other way, but most examiners will work with you. They want you to be safe. They want you to have the knowledge.

Kenny Keller & Dan "Taz" Christman

Chapter 9
Answer like you are in court

Gary is a retired police officer. I'm an ex-cop, and I learned this from being in law enforcement. You go to court routinely. That's what you do. You are taught as a police officer to only answer the question that you've been asked. Don't elaborate. Don't try to prove your point. The more you talk, the worse it is going to go in court. It's the same way with a checkride.

One of the best checkrides I've ever seen was with my good friend, Dr. Nick, who has the Enstrom that we fly six months of the year. I prepped him with this tip. He's a doctor, and he understands about going to court. He's a smart guy, and he listened to what I told him.

He had one of the best checkrides ever because every time the examiner would ask him a question, Nick would pause for a few seconds and think before answering. The examiner would move on to the next question. Nick would again pause and think before he answered. He took five or ten seconds before opening his mouth, and that is the best way to do it.

I've seen other people who would respond to the same question, "What is retreating blade stall?" And very quickly say things like, "Oh, well, when you've got this advancing blade, and you've got a retreating blade, and the advancing blade is going up, and retreating blade is going down. And because of this difference in lift, and…"

If you do that, you are digging your own hole with the examiner, and he's going to say, "Tell me about that advancing blade. Tell me about that retreating blade." He's going to nail you. Don't give him everything.

If you go in there all excited and want to show that examiner that you've been studying and what you know, it will be just like being a cop in court who wants to add, "Yeah, but this guy is a dirt bag, and he's been arrested ten times before." You want to just tell everything, but you can't do that. On the checkride you've got to answer like you're in court. Answer like you're protecting your own family member, and you are doing it within the limits of the law by saying, "Yep. Nope." Just give the shortest answer possible.

Chapter 10
I failed my first helicopter checkride

I failed my first helicopter check ride and today I make my living because of that failure. We're all scared of failing. Nobody wants to fail. Is it the worst thing that is ever going to happen to you in your life? No. Does it suck? Yeah. It sucks. But I did. I failed.

In turn, I created what I do today online. I failed my first checkride. I know what it's like. I went home for six months with my tail between my legs. I didn't even know if I was ever going to finish. I was out working as a cop and one of my cop buddies, a guy I was training, asked me when I was going to finish that rating. I'm like, "You know what? I need to do it."

He said, "Well, yeah. All that time and effort."

That's when I created the notebook that I talk about all the time, and I started studying my butt off. I went back, and I nailed it the second time around. And when I got my first job, they very quickly caught on to how good I was with the regulations and how good I was with all the ground knowledge. It isn't because I'm so smart. It's because I failed, and I was going to go back and do it and not fail the second time around. About halfway through the oral with a different examiner, he said, "Hey Kenny, why did you fail your first time around? You came in here with a pink slip today.

I said, "Because I didn't know my stuff then like I know it now." He told me that I was batting 100% and answering everything. And I told him that it was because I applied myself.

And he said, "You know what? I'm going to contact this guy that you took your first checkride with, and I am going to personally tell him how well you did when you came back so that he knows that you did end up finishing and that you did really well."

After my first failure, the examiner said, "You have to know your stuff. I do not want to come to your helicopter accident. If you are struggling to answer me across the table during the oral portion of your test, I don't know what you're going to be doing when you are out there in the aircraft."

Chapter 11
Additional

I took my first checkride with the FAA. Another tip is to take it with a designated examiner. It sounds bad but at the FAA guy gets paid to just come and give you a checkride. A designated examiner is designated by the FAA but doesn't work for the FAA. He gets paid by you. He is still required to have you do everything within tolerance, but in general, an FAA examiner is probably going to be tougher. You can use the FAA examiner for free.

But I failed. I've had only three people fail in 20 years. It has been a long time. One of them became a good friend of mine. He is a medical doctor who had never failed at anything in his life. He got himself freaked out the day of the checkride, and he choked. He got through the oral, but even during the oral, he struggled. The examiner came out and said, "Man, your boy is struggling."
I said, "Well, you know. He was an add-on pilot and was recently flight-reviewed, so he kept giving me the attitude of 'Well, I just did

my flight review, so I'm good on all this ground stuff.'" I would remind him to just be careful.

He ended up failing his checkride. I didn't hear from him for a while. This guy's wife called me at home and said, "Kenny, you have got to get a hold of my husband. He has never failed at anything in his life, and he is devastated." She said that he was moping around the house and being a jerk at home. She wanted me to get him back in there and make him finish because she was having a hard time living with him like that. Fortunately he is still married all these years later!

I called him up and said, "Man, get back in here and let's finish this thing up." All we had to do was go out and freshen up the autorotation. That's all he had to do. He just had to do an autorotation to finish. In the end, we got him done. He got the rating, and it was no big deal the second time around. The pressure is off when you go back in to retest. The oral was done. All those other maneuvers were done for him. All he had to do that day was hop in with the examiner and go do an auto. That's it.

He's still a friend of mine, but he said to me, "I'm only going to say this to you one time, Kenny. From now on when you work with add-on guys, you make sure that they know all the VFR stuff. Make sure you go back through everything with them."

I said, "You know I tried doing that with you, and you had to tell me how you just did your biannual flight review in the airplanes. And whenever I would talk about basic VFR stuff, you'd always kind of blow me off, so I'm putting part of this back on you."

And he replied, "Well, I'll never say it again. But I'm just telling you to make sure you go through everything with add-on pilots."

I use that today when somebody asks if I have a course just for an add-on. The answer is, "No. You need to go through everything, even if you are an add-on." It's fair game, and let's make that **Bonus Tip, Add-on pilots still need to know basic VFR.** If you fly a lot of IFR and come to me and tell me you're an IFR guy and you're ready to go but you've got a checkride coming up so you just need a couple of hours, the first thing I'm going to do is open up a sectional chart and start asking you VFR stuff. Nine times out of ten I'm going to trip you up if you fly a lot of IFR because you get complacent. When you just fly IFR all the time, the VFR skills many times go out the window.

Gary also reminded us that most examiners will keep asking you questions to the point where you must look something up. It is key to remember to not say, "I don't know." Do not sit back and give up like that. You have all your documents with you. You've got your FAR/AIM and your helicopter flying handbook. You should say something to the effect of, "You know, darn it. I just read that. I can look it up for you."

We need to know how to find things for the examiner. That's not going to add up to a failure. He wants to see that you can find things anyway. That's why he's taking you to the point of having to look something up. He will take it until he can stump you or until he can teach you something.

There are a couple different ways that examiners are operating. Some are using scenarios instead of the traditional questions about helicopter aerodynamics. Be ready. You might go down through some accidents, read them, and see if you can figure out what happened with that accident without reading what the FAA has determined to be the cause.

You need to know the specifics of the aircraft, that you are actually flying in, for that ride. Look through that POH and know the specs on it. Know what the POH has to say for handling all the emergencies, because each aircraft can be slightly different.

Chapter 12
From The Examiners...

During the research for this book, Taz talked to several examiners from the Las Vegas area to see some of the checkride trends are that they are experiencing. This chapter is more on specifics the DPEs are seeing during the flight portion. They are listed here in no particular order.

During the navigation portion, the PTS says the pilot must compute time to a waypoint and corrects for differences between preflight fuel, groundspeed and heading. They must do this within 3 NM of planned route and within 5 minutes of ETA. On almost every flight, the applicant forgets to start the time for the legs of their cross-country flight, so it makes it difficult to judge any correction if the student forgets to start their timer.

Believe it or not a lot of applicants have a tough time with radio communication and traffic pattern entry. This probably stems from the CFI doing too much for the student during dual flight instruction.

PTS Area of Operation III: Task A: Radio Communication and ATC Light Signals states that the applicant must:
1. Exhibits knowledge of the elements related to radio communications and ATC light signals.
2. Selects appropriate frequencies.
3. Transmits using recommended phraseology.
4. Acknowledges radio communications and compiles with instructions.

The airspace around Las Vegas is extremely busy at times and saturated with aircraft. There is an established frequency to be used in the training area for deconfliction. A lot of students forget to switch to this practice area frequency. Some students only make one or two position reports or sometimes none at all. Remember there are 10 Special Emphasis Areas that the examiners are required to place special emphasis on because they are considered critical to flight safety. Not only does this not follow local radio procedures but it also violates One of the SEAs, collision avoidance.

Most of the airports in the Vegas valley are Class D airports. Students tend to switch back to tower and skip ATIS assuming that it has not changed, which is not the correct procedure. Controllers may issue instructions that the student might miss or not fully understand. Rather than ask the control to repeat, the student will sometimes ask, "what did they say?" Remember that the examiner is simply a passenger and the applicant is the PIC so the examiner can't help them.

The examiners understand that students are nervous, but it is important that they listen to the examiners instructions. For example, an examiner will be planning on testing settling with power. They will instruct the student to climb to 1500 - 2000' AGL and clear the area. Then they tell them to bring the airspeed to 0 and do a HOGE. They assume they are going to do settling with power so they just do settling with power procedure. The examiner will then ask them why they got into settling with power when all they asked for was a HOGE.

Another example of this is quick stops. Sometimes during the takeoff the examiner might say "pretend a plane just pulled out in front of us and you need to do a quick stop". A lot of CFIs only teach quick stops at 40 ft and 40 knots. So the applicant continues to accelerate, which causes them to "crash into the pretend plane". When asked why they continued accelerating when asked to do a quick stop. They answer, "well, we do quick stops from 40 ft and 40 knots".

Even though the performance maneuvers listed in the PTS are Straight in Autorotation and the 180 Autorotation, its important that CFI's also train students to do 90 degree autos, and 104 degree autos, etc. During the Emergency operations they will be tested on Power Failure at Altitude. You never know how many degrees you will need to turn to get into the wind and find a suitable landing spots, so practice autos with turns, not just the straight in and 180 auto.

Finally, during the max performance takeoff make sure to check the mags and talk about dynamic rollover if in an off-airport landing environment. Slope landings are "rushed" a lot of the time so make sure to take your time.

Top Ten Checkride Tips

APPLICANT'S PRACTICAL TEST CHECKLIST
APPOINTMENT WITH EXAMINER:

ACCEPTABLE AIRCRAFT
- ☐ Aircraft Documents:
    Airworthiness Certificate
    Registration Certificate
    Operating Limitations
- ☐ Aircraft Maintenance Records:
    Logbook Record of Airworthiness Inspections
    and AD Compliance
- ☐ Pilot's Operating Handbook and FAA-Approved
    Helicopter Flight Manual
- ☐ FCC Station License (if applicable)

PERSONAL EQUIPMENT
- ☐ Current Aeronautical Charts
- ☐ Computer and Plotter
- ☐ Flight Plan Form
- ☐ Flight Logs
- ☐ Current AIM, Airport Facility Directory, and Appropriate
- ☐ Publications

PERSONAL RECORDS
- ☐ Identification—Photo/Signature ID
- ☐ Pilot Certificate
- ☐ Current and Appropriate Medical Certificate
- ☐ Completed FAA Form 8710-1, Airman Certificate and/or
- ☐ Rating Application with Instructor's Signature (if
- ☐ applicable)
- ☐ AC Form 8080-2, Airman Written Test Report or
- ☐ Computer Test Report
- ☐ Pilot Logbook with Appropriate Instructor Endorsements
- ☐ FAA Form 8060-5, Notice of Disapproval (if applicable)
- ☐ Approved School Graduation Certificate (if applicable)
- ☐ Examiner's Fee (if applicable)

ABOUT THE AUTHORS

Kenny Keller

Created, developed and presented by Amazon No. 1 Best Selling Author Kenny Keller, a former law enforcement officer, now a skilled Helicopter Certified Flight Instructor, Instrument Rated Commercial Pilot, Remote Pilot and the creator of Helicopter Online Ground School, with 20 years of aviation experience. Captain Keller has a reputation for being 'passionate, loyal and reliable'. When it comes to quality check-ride training and ground school instruction, you're in the right place.

Dan "Taz" Christman

2018 National Certificated Flight Instructor of the Year

From the General Aviation Awards page at:

http://www.generalaviationawards.com/award-winners/

Daniel Peter Christman of Las Vegas, Nevada has been named the 2018 National Certificated Flight Instructor of the Year. As a young kid growing up in northern Indiana, Dan always knew he wanted to be a pilot. His father was in the Air Force Reserves and would regularly take Dan to the base to see the planes. When he was 11 his parents bribed him, saying that if he made the honor roll they would get him some flying lessons. It worked, and he has been hooked ever since.

Dan soloed on his 16th birthday and received his Private Pilot certificate a year later at age 17. Since then, he's earned the following certificates: Air Transport Pilot multiengine land, Commercial Pilot single engine land and sea, instrument helicopter and glider, Flight Instructor single and multiengine, instrument airplane, helicopter, instrument helicopter and glider, Ground Instructor advanced and instrument, Flight Engineer turbojet, and Remote Pilot small UAS.

Dan's day job is as a Lieutenant Colonel in the USAF—where he's known as "Taz"—presently serving as Deputy Commander of the Persistent Attack and Reconnaissance Operations Center at Creech AFB, as well as a military instructor/evaluator pilot. His military flight experience includes the Northrop T-38A/C Talon jet trainer, Rockwell B-1B Lancer bomber, and General Atomics MQ-9 Reaper remotely-piloted aircraft (RPA).

Teaching flying is clearly Dan's passion. In addition to his full-time duties with the Air Force, Dan averages 25-30 hours of flight instruction a month and another 10-15 hours of ground training per week. He has been an active flight instructor either full or part-time for over 19 years with more than 5,000 hours of dual instruction given in a diverse array of aircraft. Dan's experience and teaching style make him a highly sought-after instructor. As a part-time instructor with Airwork Las Vegas, he currently has six full-time and four part-time flight students plus five ground school students. He currently has a two-month waiting list for any new prospective students. As Airwork's chief flight instructor, he's responsible for managing 8 instructors and 25 students.

Dan authored and instructed a 6-week Private Pilot and Instrument ground school for both Airplane and Helicopter's through UNLV's continuing education program. He was instrumental in writing, producing, and instructing an ATP Flight/Ground School for Sin City Flying Club which produced over 60 ATP certifications during the last two years. Dan created the first aerobatic/upset recovery training program in the region utilizing Decathlon and Yak-52 aircraft. He is an experienced Technically Advanced Aircraft (TAA) instructor specializing in Avidyne, Garmin, Aspen and Honeywell glass cockpits.

He created and recorded over 55 hours of video content for Helicopter Online Ground School (HOGS) Instrument Rating course.

Dan is also a contributing instructor for a weekly free live streaming helicopter safety and education course available on YouTube the HOGS website.

A favorite saying of Dan's is; "An empty seat is a missed opportunity". What he's referring to is any time after you're a certificated pilot that you fly solo, it's a missed opportunity to share aviation with someone. Dan is a huge proponent of the Young Eagles program and will routinely share his love for aviation with younger kids, trying to pass on the experiences of his own youth. As an aviation ambassador to young enlisted Air Force airmen, Taz designed an incentive ride program to help motivate them to become officers and pilots. He personally flew 19 enlisted airmen free of charge in personal aircraft, three of whom decided to start flight training. dan@chrisair.net

Made in the USA
Columbia, SC
16 February 2019